STACCATO SCRIPTS

ANNIE KENNEY

Alan Plater

Series Editors/Support Material:
Kate Harris and John Mannion

Stanley Thornes (Publishers) Ltd

First published in 1991 by:
Stanley Thornes (Publishers) Ltd
Old Station Drive
Leckhampton
CHELTENHAM GL53 0DN
England

British Library Cataloguing in Publication Data

Plater, Alan
Annie Kenney. — (Staccato scripts)
I. Title II. Series
822

ISBN 0 7487 1165 1

Typeset by Tech-Set, Gateshead Tyne and Wear
Printed and bound in Great Britain at Ebenezer Baylis & Son Ltd
The Trinity Press, Worcester and London.

ACKNOWLEDGEMENTS

The authors and publishers are grateful to the following for permission to reproduce extracts and photographs:

Barnaby's Picture Library page 35 ● Century Hutchinson, *Unshackled,* Christabel Pankhurst pages 44–7 ● *The Independent* page 54 ● Andrew Lambert page 36 ● Mary Evans Picture Library pages 36, 43, 45, 47, 51, 53, 56, 57 ● Museum of London pages 41, 49, 52 ● Topham Picture Library pages 54, 55.

The publishers have made every effort to contact copyright holders and apologise if any have been overlooked.

CONTENTS

CHARACTERS

Annie Kenney
Mrs Kenney
Jessie Kenney
Chatterton
Christabel Pankhurst
Mrs Pankhurst
Sylvia Pankhurst
Teresa Billington
Charlie
Chairman
Bell
Halliday
Carrick
Flora Drummond
Mrs Roe
Keir Hardie
Frederick Pethick Lawrence
Emmeline Pethick Lawrence
Mary
Accompanist
Butler
Spectators at fairground
Stewards and **Spectators** at Free Trade Hall
Magistrates and **Spectators** in courtroom
Prison Warder and **Prisoners**
Guests at Nelson Street
Committee Members
Tramps on the Embankment
Audience at Caxton Hall
Choir

THE PLAY

Scene: **A Pennine valley**. *It is a hard, beautiful and useful landscape. As we view the valley, we hear the singing of the* **Choir**.

Choir 'From street and square, from hill and glen,
Of this vast world beyond my door,
I hear the tread of marching men,
The patient armies of the poor.

'Not ermine-clad or clothed in state,
Their title-deeds not yet made plain,
But waking early, toiling late,
The heirs of all the earth remain.'

(*Huddled in the valley is a small town which is dominated by the spiky outlines of the cotton mill. As we look at the mill the sound of the* **Choir** *drops in volume and* **Annie Kenney's** *voice can be heard over the music*)

Choir (*Though we will not hear the words*)
'The peasant brain shall yet be wise,
The untamed pulse grow calm and still;
And blind shall see, the lowly rise,
And work in peace Time's wondrous will.'

Annie A big family, the Kenneys. Eleven of us. I'm the fifth. We live in a village in the valley.

(*Beyond the mill chimneys there is a hillside on which we see a cluster of tiny figures – a long way away but they look like children*)

Sunday afternoons we'd go for long walks and sometimes people thought we were a Sunday School outing, so many of us. We'd walk for miles to see the first spring flowers. Then in the evening. . .

Scene: **The Kenney living room.** *In the light of an oil lamp,* **Mrs Kenney** *reads to her family. She is a fine, bold, working-class aristocrat: the dignity and the signs of wear-and-tear both apparent on her face. The children are in shadow.* **Annie's** *narration continues over this scene.*

Annie My mother would read to us. Somehow, the stories were always about the poor people who live in London. . . .

(**Mrs Kenney** *is reading the story*)

Mrs Kenney 'The alley into which he turned might, for filth and misery, have competed with the darkest corner of this ancient sanctury in its dirtiest and most lawless time. The houses, varying from two storeys in height to four, were stained with every indescribable hue that long exposure to the weather, damp and rottenness can impart to tenements composed originally of the roughest and coarsest materials. The windows were patched with paper, and stuffed with the foulest rags; the doors were hanging on their hinges; poles with lines on which to dry clothes projected from every casement, and sounds of quarrelling and drunkenness issued from every room.'

(**Mrs Kenney** *continues her reading in the background as we hear* **Annie's** *voice over*)

Annie I think it was my mother's idea that my sister and I should join the choir. . . . It wasn't my idea, because I can't sing. . . .

(*The sound of* **The Choir** *fades under* **Annie's** *words and then comes in loud and hard when she stops speaking*)

Scene: **The Co-Op hall.** *A small clean, unpretentious hall in Oldham.* **The Choir** *is assembled on a stage. Behind them a large banner reads:* Oldham Clarion Vocal Union. **Annie** *and her sister,* **Jessie,** *are in the choir;* **Annie** *sings with great enthusiasm – though there might be some question about whether any sound is actually emerging.*

Choir 'Some day, without a trumpet call,
The news will o'er the world be blown:
The heritage comes back to all;
The myriad monarchs take their own.'

(*There is a brief pause, then* **Chatterton,** *the conductor, smiles his approval*)

Chatterton Thank you all very much, that was splendid. You've earned a short rest, while I try to remember where I put the new music. . . .

(*He crosses to the piano and flips his way through a pile of untidy stacked music. In the meantime,* **Annie** *and* **Jessie** *talk*)

Jessie Annie. . . .

Annie Yes, love. . . .

Jessie Are you free next Thursday evening?

Annie I'm not sure. Mr Balfour promised to take me out to dinner at the Midland but. . . .

Jessie Tory prime ministers always let you down, you know that. . . .

Annie Is it something exciting?

Jessie Jane's invited us to a special meeting of the Oldham Trades Council.

(**Annie** *is not all that impressed*)

Annie What's special about it?

Jessie They've got two guest speakers coming. . . .

Annie Who?

Jessie Teresa Billington and Christabel Pankhurst. Talking about women's suffrage. . . .

Annie Christabel? That's Mrs Pankhurst's daughter . . . ?

Jessie Yes.

Annie I heard her mother speak once . . . I didn't really understand what she was talking about. . . .

(*The opening bars of the next song for rehearsal are played on the piano*)

Chatterton Back to work, please. We'll sing 'The Patriot's Hymn'. . . .

Annie (*to* **Jessie**) I'll come if it isn't raining. . . .

(**Chatterton** *leads them into song*)

Scene: **The Co-Op hall** *meeting. The same setting, but a different occasion. A group of people, including* **Annie,** *is sitting at the front of the audience applauding enthusiastically. On the stage,* **Christabel Pankhurst** *speaks. The small platform party includes* **Teresa Billington.**

Christabel Now . . . we have been accused, not without reason, of being a middle-class organisation pursuing middle-class aims. Let me deny the accusation here and now. This is a much bigger battle on a much larger battlefield. Consider the average middle-class lady of leisure. She is warm. She is comfortable and well fed. She has a husband to work for her, and servants to save her from soiling her hands. Tell her she is disenfranchised, she will wonder what the word means . . . and be much too polite to ask. (*Some laughter from the audience, but* **Annie** *listens hard*) Consider the working-class woman. She brings up her own children, looks after her husband, cleans the house . . . and very likely works a long shift at the mill as well. . . . Isn't this the woman who is entitled to a say in how the world . . . *her* world . . . is organised? In the words of the poet, 'We're far too low to vote the tax, But we're not too low to pay.' (*Applause*) In the past we have said to our governments: 'Are you in favour of women having the vote?' And they smile, nod their heads gravely, and agree: Yes, they are in favour . . . but unfortunately they have other, more pressing problems . . . an election to win or a war to fight . . . and women must take their turn. This year, next year, sometime, never. . . . So now we have changed the question. Now the question is: 'Will you give us the vote?' And we will demand the answer: Yes.

(**Christabel** *sits down. There is a brief pause then enthusiastic applause.* **Annie,** *staring at* **Christabel,** *joins in louder than anybody. The room fills with lively, after-the-show informal chatter as the speakers and the audience drink tea.* **Annie** *makes her way through the groups of people towards* **Christabel.**)

Annie Miss Pankhurst. . . .

Christabel Yes?

Annie I just wanted to say how much I enjoyed your speech.

Christabel I'm not so much concerned with enjoyment. Did you agree with it?

Annie Every word.

Christabel What can you do to help us?

Annie Help?

Christabel I'm not interested in people who smile, nod their heads gravely and walk away. . . .

Annie You said that in the speech.

Christabel We're the new kind of politicians. . . . We say the same things up there (*She indicates the platform*) . . . and down here.

(*Pause*)

Annie I work in a mill . . . and I'm active in the trade union . . . so there's nothing to stop me organising a meeting . . . a lot of meetings if you like . . . for the factory women, the working women.

(*There is a sense that* **Annie** *is thinking on her feet*; **Christabel** *has done her thinking long before she arrived here*)

Christabel What's your name, dear?

Annie Annie. Annie Kenney.

Christabel Annie to your friends?

Annie Yes.

Christabel I'm Christabel to mine.

(*They shake hands: it's an affirmation, more than a token*)

Scene: **The Pankhursts' sitting-room at Nelson Street. Christabel** *is introducing* **Annie** *to the assembled Sunday afternoon company:* **Mrs Pankhurst, Teresa Billington, Sylvia Pankhurst** *and others. The introductions begin, predictably, with* **Mrs Pankhurst**

Christabel My mother.

Mrs Pankhurst How lovely to meet you my dear. Christabel tells me you're going to work miracles for us on the factory floor.

Annie (*Optimistic, as always*) I'll do my best.

Christabel My sister, Sylvia.

Sylvia Hello, Annie . . .

Annie Pleased to meet you, Miss Pankhurst.

Sylvia (*Gently correcting*) Sylvia.

Mrs Pankhurst Sylvia's studying in London but she's come home for the weekend to collect her secret political orders.

Christabel Teresa Billington you met the other evening . . .

Teresa But everybody calls me Tess. Total lack of respect, you see.

Annie There used to be a dog in the village called Tess.

Teresa (*To Christabel*) I always come when I'm called . . . correct?

Christabel Always.

(*A quiet bubble of laughter into which* **Mrs Pankhurst** *issues her next instruction*)

Mrs Pankhurst Now you must tell us all about yourself, Annie. (*She beckons* **Annie** *to join her in a chair next to hers by the fireplace.* **Annie** *does so, and sits*)

Annie Everything?

Mrs Pankhurst Everything.

Annie Can I leave out the rude bits? (*Laughter. A pause, then* **Annie** *starts her story – the words are the same as those which opened the play*) Well . . . A big family, the Kenneys. Eleven of us. I'm the fifth.

Scene: **The Pennine valley**. *The conversation from the previous scene continues into this different setting. We see the valley and hear* **Annie's** *voice.*

Annie We live in a village in the valley.

(**Annie** *and* **Christabel** *walk across a field overlooking the valley*)

Christabel Is that where you work?

Annie Where the chimneys stand, yes. I started part-time when I was ten. Full-time when I was thirteen.

Christabel Sweated labour, as Sylvia would say.

Annie It sometimes got a bit warm.

Christabel So you started work in the trade union movement.

Annie I talk too much, that's all. If the girls wanted a spokesman, they'd pick on the one that talked too much. Sensible people keep quiet and walk away. Not me. The mouth keeps flying open and the words pour out. It can be a nuisance.

(**Christabel** *laughs, delighted with* **Annie's** *company, as they walk on. They come to a dry-stone wall overlooking a breath-taking landscape and sit down*)

Christabel Your mother sounds like a marvellous woman.

Annie Was.

Christabel I'm sorry . . . ?

Annie She died at the beginning of the year. (*Pause*) I miss her a lot. We were very close. A bit like you and your mother, I think . . . (**Christabel** *nods quiet agreement*) I miss her a lot, that's why I'd like to do something for her. A struggle, eleven of us to bring up, always a struggle. Yes, I'd like to do something.

Christabel I liked your story about her reading to you on Sunday evenings.

Annie Not a story. That was true. And she encouraged us to read . . . the house is full of books . . . Tom Paine, Carpenter, Blatchford, Walt Whitman. . . .

Christabel We've got the same books. . . . (*Pause*) Every time we go walking, we must bring a notebook and pencil. Write down all the important ideas we discuss. Do you agree?

Annie I don't have many ideas. Mostly I remember other people's. But yes . . . I agree. (*Pause*) One thing you could write down . . . if you had a notebook.

Christabel What's that?

Annie Dates. The dates of the meetings I'm organising.

(**Christabel** *is delighted and surprised that* **Annie** *is moving so quickly*)

Scene: **A fairground.** *We hear a steam organ playing in the background. We are on the edge of a Wakes Week fairground. A cart is drawn up and decked with a homemade banner reading:* Votes for Women. **Annie** *stands on the cart addressing the audience of about half a dozen. Other passers-by pause as they go past but for them and for most of the watchers,* **Annie** *is just another sideshow.*

Annie I'm speaking for the women who work in the mills . . . the weavers, card-room workers, ring spinners, winders and reelers . . . working ten hours a day then going home to look after a husband, a home and a house full of children. . . . And I'm speaking for the women who work in the sweated home trades . . . fourteen hours a day for six shillings a week. *That's* the world men have made for us. *That's* the world we're going to put right when we get the vote.

(*In the crowd is an amiably boozed-up man,* **Charlie**)

Charlie Question, missus. . . .

Annie I'll answer any questions. . . .

(*With prospects of some fun brewing, the crowd swells to about a dozen*)

Charlie What about horses?

Annie What *about* horses?

Charlie Why shouldn't horses have the vote? That horse of yours talks more sense than you do.

(*Laughter*)

Annie Aye, and I bet he works harder than *you* do. Mind you, he doesn't drink as much. . . .

(*More laughter.* **Annie** *has obviously won this round*)

Charlie I'll tell you this, missus . . . if I was married to you, I'd push you off Blackpool Tower.

Annie If I was married to *you*, mister, I'd jump off Blackpool Tower.

(*She wins herself a round of applause*)

Scene: **The sitting-room at Nelson Street. Mrs Pankhurst, Christabel, Annie** *and* **Teresa Billington** *are present. The room is now more of a committee room or campaign HQ than a social setting.*

Mrs Pankhurst I keep hearing very exciting reports of the work you're doing, Annie . . .

Annie I've only had one black eye so far . . . (**Mrs Pankhurst** *is looking at a press cutting, apparently about one of* **Annie's** *meetings*) And you mustn't believe everything they put in the papers.

Mrs Pankhurst I don't. I believe what my daughter tells me.

Teresa What happened in Oldham?

Annie If the choir hadn't been there, there wouldn't have been an audience at all.

Christabel There were other people there besides the choir . . .

Annie Two friends of my sister's and a tabby cat that came in after a mouse. You didn't see the mouse, did you?

Teresa A mouse? I'm glad I wasn't there.

Annie Can be a hard life in Oldham.

Mrs Pankhurst There'll be no mice at the Free Trade Hall.

Christabel (*To her mother*) Except on the platform.

Annie The Free Trade Hall? We're not having a meeting at the Free Trade Hall, are we?

Christabel Not us. The Liberals.

Mrs Pankhurst Winston Churchill and Sir Edward Grey . . . rousing the electorate ready for the General Election.

Annie I shan't go to that. I've heard it all before.

Teresa We all have.

Christabel You're going, Annie, and so am I.

Annie Is it compulsory?

Mrs Pankhurst Somebody has to ask the question.

Annie Question?

(**Mrs Pankhurst** *hands* **Annie** *a piece of paper*)

Annie (*Reads*) 'If you are elected, will you do your best to make Woman Suffrage a Government measure?'

Teresa It's a very cunning question.

Annie Is it?

Mrs Pankhurst If Churchill says yes, the Government will be committed. If he says no, the Liberal women will want to know the reason why.

(**Annie** *looks at* **Christabel**)

Annie Is it your question?

Mrs Pankhurst Christabel's question, yes.

Annie What if they ignore us? Or just refuse to answer?

Christabel We have to *make* them answer.

Annie We ask the question. And then we see what happens next . . . we might have to think fast. . . .

Christabel That's why. . . .

Annie (*Finishing the sentence with* **Christabel**) That's why *we're* going. . . .

Mrs Pankhurst You're not frightened, are you?

Annie If I can run meetings at pit heads and factory gates, a hall full of Liberals won't be any trouble. . . .

Mrs Pankhurst But you must understand the real reason, Annie. . . . You know I'm a working woman, too.

Annie I know you're the breadwinner, Mrs Pankhurst. . . .

Mrs Pankhurst I've been threatened by my employers – if I continue to involve myself in political activities they will dismiss me. I'm happy to ignore the threat, except that I must use a little discretion. . . .

Annie No shouting from the gallery at the Free Trade Hall.

Mrs Pankhurst Straight to the heart of the problem, as usual.

Annie I don't mind. I'll shout at anybody. The cause will be in good hands.

Mrs Pankhurst I know.

Annie Christabel, I mean. . . .

Mrs Pankhurst Yes, the finest hands.

(*Pause*)

Annie Christabel's not frightened of the Liberals, are you?

Christabel No. Are you?

Annie Me? I'm not frightened of anybody.

(*This is a simple statement of fact*)

Scene: **The Free Trade Hall.** *In the centre of the stage sits the* **Chairman** *of the meeting; in the gallery are* **Annie** *and* **Christabel.** *These central characters are surrounded by the noise of the gathering – everybody talking and nobody listening.*

Chairman Next question, please. . . .

Annie If you are elected, will you do your best to make Woman Suffrage a Government measure?

Chairman May we have the next question, please . . . yes?

Christabel You haven't answered our question.

Annie If you are elected, will you do your best to make Woman Suffrage a Government measure?

(*There are shouts of* 'Answer the question!' *and counter-shouts of* 'Throw them out!')

Chairman Gentleman at the back of the hall, downstairs. . . .

Annie If you are elected, will you do your best to make Woman Suffrage a Government measure?

Chairman May we have your question, sir? (*He gives a quiet, gentlemanly signal to the* **Stewards**) Yes, you, sir. . . .

(*Three or four* **Stewards** *come into the gallery and try to grab the girls. They struggle and unfurl their* 'Vote for Women' *banners. The noise from the hall grows as the two girls continue to shout*)

Christabel What are you frightened of? What is the Liberal Party frightened of?

Annie If you are elected, will you do your best to make Woman Suffrage a Government measure?

Christabel (*To audience*) Are you prepared to see this happening in your country? In the land of the free?

Chairman May we please have order in the hall, please! (*He bangs on the table*) Thank you, gentlemen.

(*The* **Stewards** *drag and push* **Annie** *and* **Christabel** *towards the exit doors*)

Annie Yes or No? Will you give us the vote? Yes or No?

(*She is forced out the door to cheers and boos from the audience*)

Scene: **A magistrates' court.** *Although the court is crowded and excited, this is a sharp contrast to the previous scene. On the magisterial bench there are five magistrates including* **Halliday,** *the chairman.* **Christabel** *and* **Annie** *are in the dock.* **Mrs Pankhurst, Teresa Billington** *and others seen at Nelson Street are in the public gallery.* **Carrick,** *a reporter, is among the pressmen.* **Robert Bell** *outlines the case for the prosecution.*

Bell Miss Kenney and Miss Pankhurst are charged with disorderly behaviour in the street and Miss Pankhurst is also charged with assaulting the police. (*Pause*) If the evidence is true, the defendants have behaved more like women from the slums. (**Annie** *is stung by this*) In spite of this, there is no desire that a heavy penalty should be inflicted, but the magistrates will be asked to take such means as to prevent a recurrence of such a scene.

(**Bell** *sits down. There is a passage of time.* **Annie** *waves to* **Teresa; Carrick** *works on his notes;* **Halliday** *has a mysterious whispered conversation with his colleagues.* **Christabel** *stands up to address the court*)

Christabel In defence of my actions, I believe they were justified because of the treatment I received at the hands of Sir Edward Grey and the other speakers at the Free Trade Hall. At the time I assaulted the police officers, I was not aware that they *were* police officers. I thought they were Liberals.

(*There is laughter in the court, notably a big guffaw from* **Annie**)

Halliday Quiet, please.

Christabel My deepest regret is that one of the men I assaulted was not Sir Edward himself. I stand by my every action and will do so again.

(*There is a smattering of applause from the public gallery*)

Halliday (*Breaking in*) Thank you, Miss Pankhurst.

(**Christabel** *sits down again. Again there is a passage of time.* **Teresa** *and* **Mrs Pankhurst** *talk*)

Teresa I thought Christabel was absolutely splendid.

Mrs Pankhurst Is she ever anything less?

Teresa I suppose not. (*She looks towards* **Annie**) I wonder whether Annie. . . .

Mrs Pankhurst Annie will also be absolutely splendid.

(**Annie** *stands up*)

Annie I am a mill worker, a representative of the local card-room hands' association and am currently assisting in the organisation of women workers for the Independent Labour Party. I went to the meeting on behalf of those women . . . as a representative of thousands of British working women, to ask certain questions of Sir Edward Grey. . . .

Halliday We are not concerned with Sir Edward Grey.

Annie Sir, I am very concerned with Sir Edward Grey . . . if it wasn't for Sir Edward Grey I wouldn't be standing here in this court. . . .

Halliday Will you please limit yourself to the charges.

Annie I'm sorry. What am I charged with? I've forgotten with all the excitement. . . .

Halliday Obstructing the police.

Annie I *might* have obstructed some people and they might have been policemen. On the other hand, a lot of people obstructed me. I was hustled out of the hall. I was treated very roughly. They might have been policemen but I had no way of telling. In any case, I have no regrets about anything I did. I was acting on behalf of the working women of this country. I will do it all again, if necessary.

(**Annie** *sits down, again to a smattering of applause from the public gallery*)

Christabel Well done.

Annie Thank you.

Christabel I wonder what they'll do to us?

Annie Deportation, I should think.

Christabel They're going away to decide. (*Pause*) But whatever it is, we're ready for them.

(*They stand along with the rest of the court as the* **Magistrates** *leave. They sit.* **Carrick** *walks past the dock and stops for a quick word*)

Carrick Miss Pankhurst?

Christabel Yes?

Carrick Carrick . . . *Evening Chronicle* . . . may I have a word with you?

Christabel On the strict understanding that you write down exactly what I say.

Annie And we still think it's all Sir Edward Grey's fault.

(*Again we move on in time. Then* **Annie** *and* **Christabel** *stand in the dock as* **Halliday** *announces the magistrates' decision*)

Halliday Miss Pankhurst will be fined ten shillings for assaulting the police with the alternative of seven days' imprisonment. Miss Pankhurst and Miss Kenney will be fined five shillings each for obstructing the police, with the alternative of three days' imprisonment. The sentences will be concurrent in the case of Miss Pankhurst.

Christabel I shall pay no fine.

Halliday Have you any goods to distrain upon?

Christabel I think not.

Halliday Miss Kenney?

Annie I refuse to pay any fine. And I am without goods.

Halliday You both know the alternative.

Scene: **The prison visitors' room at Strangeways. Jessie** *crosses the room and sits down to talk to* **Annie.** There is a **Warder** *in attendance.* **Jessie** *is more disturbed by the experience than* **Annie**)

Jessie Annie. . . .

Annie Hello, Jessie. . . . (*She is very cheerful*) Good of you to call in. . . .

Jessie I've got some money to pay the fine.

Annie I don't want anybody to pay the fine.

Jessie That's why I thought I'd ask you first.

Annie Good girl. (*Pause*) Spend it on a good cause, put it in the missionary box if you like.

Jessie It said in the paper Winston Churchill wanted to pay the fines. . . .

Annie Save the honour of the Liberal Party.

Jessie I suppose so.

Annie And his seat at the General Election. No, you see, Jessie . . . if we'd paid the fine . . . or if we'd gone home peacefully like they asked us . . . there'd be nothing in the papers at all. Couple of paragraphs, perhaps. But this way. . . .

Jessie The prison way?

Annie Yes.

Jessie What's it really like?

(*Pause*)

Annie It's very strange. You know it's only for three days. They tell you it's only for three days . . . but you fret . . . you wonder. You wonder whether they might forget what they said. That's the worst part. You feel forgotten. Will they remember at the end of three days? Will they remember to let you out? (*A pause; then* **Annie** *recovers her spirits*) But when you see the others, you realise how easy it is for you. Yesterday we all had to go to chapel. . . . (*As* **Annie** *speaks we hear, quietly at first, the sound of women singing a traditional hymn; perhaps,* 'Hills of the North Rejoice') They tell you how wicked you are and there's Hell-fire and Damnation waiting if you don't repent. But we're all just women really . . . a bit sad and lost, some of them. . . . (*The singing stops abruptly.* **Annie** *and* **Jessie** *sit facing each other as before*) If I had any doubts before . . . about the movement . . . I haven't got any now. (*Pause*) What about you, love?

Jessie Me?

Annie Those who are not with us . . . must be . . .

Jessie I know the rest. (*Pause*) I'm not frightened of going to prison if you're not.

Annie You'll get your chance, my pet.

Jessie Not pet. Sister.

(*A pause before the scene ends*)

Scene: **The prison gates. Annie** *emerges from the main door of the prison along with three other* **Women** – *all three are dressed drably and poorly and look much older than their years.* **Annie** *watches them until her attention is drawn by the small reception committee awaiting her. These include* **Teresa Billington, Jessie Kenney** *and* **Mrs Pankhurst** *plus at least two bouquets of flowers and a waiting taxi. One of the other* **Women** *glances back to see what the fuss is about before she shuffles on.*

Scene: **Nelson Street. Annie** *sits by the fire eating a hearty breakfast off a tray. Close by is* **Carrick,** *the reporter.*

Annie You don't mind if I eat while I'm talking to you?

Carrick Not at all.

Annie What did you want me to say?

Carrick If you'd just tell us about your prison experiences, Miss Kenney . . .

Annie Well . . . (*A pause while she makes a bacon sandwich out of the components on the tray*) We were very well treated, I'd like to say that. No complaints about our treatment. We had to wear prison clothing, of course. But nice warm underclothes . . . not pretty but warm . . . or should I not mention that?

Carrick Mention whatever you like.

Annie They gave me a lovely pair of boots. One was too big and the other was too small. And every prisoner has to have a bath when she arrives but they thought . . . Miss Pankhurst and myself . . . it was thought we were clean enough.

Carrick What about the food?

Annie The food was fine, as long as you like porridge and brown bread. Three times on Sunday we had porridge and brown bread. Of course, sometimes they give you brown bread and porridge. Am I going too quickly?

Carrick No, you're doing fine. (*He is writing all this down eagerly, because it's good copy*)

Annie And then in church they told us not to steal, not to tell lies, not to do all sorts of things that we never do in any case, if you see what I mean. It was funny, really, but you're not allowed to laugh. (*Pause*) But no complaints. Don't forget to put that.

Carrick I won't. (*He gets up*) Thank you very much for talking to me. . . .

Annie That's all right. You haven't asked me if I'd be prepared to go back to prison. . . .

Carrick I think I know the answer to that.

Annie Good. I'm glad.

Carrick Good morning, Miss Kenney. Enjoy your breakfast.

Annie Thank you. You're very kind.

(**Carrick** *goes out, passing* **Teresa,** *who goes to join* **Annie**)

Teresa You've no idea the fuss you've caused.

Annie A good fuss or a bad fuss?

Teresa Very good. Lots of letters from all over the country. Protest meetings. There's one at the Free Trade Hall on Saturday. Keir Hardie's going to speak.

Annie Perhaps Sir Edward Grey will come and we'll be able to throw him out.

Teresa 'The brave little mill girl who's won the hearts of the country. . . .'

Annie I beg your pardon?

Teresa That's what one of the papers said . . . one that's on our side, of course. . . .

Annie Isn't it easy to get into the newspapers? (*This is a new discovery*) Mind you, I'm not sure I want to be a mill girl.

Teresa It's nothing to be ashamed of.

Annie Nobody *wants* to be a mill girl, Tess. You just get pushed into it. There's no choice.

Teresa Isn't that what the battle is all about? Women having the choice?

(*Pause*)

Annie I suppose it is. (*She smiles*) I don't know what I'd do if there weren't people around me, telling me what to think. (*Then, paradoxically, she becomes more serious as she poses her next question*) Is there any more bacon?

Scene: **A park. Annie** *and* **Christabel** *walk together.*

Christabel We have a Liberal Government with a massive majority.

Annie But Labour's won twenty-nine seats . . . that helps us, doesn't it? Keir Hardie's promised to introduce a private member's bill. . . .

Christabel He'll still need Government support . . . behind the scenes.

Annie We'll just have to carry on making a nuisance of ourselves.

Christabel Is that enough, Annie?

(**Christabel** *takes out a notebook, opens it and makes some notes*)

Annie What are you writing?

Christabel We must attack the problem at its heart. It is necessary to form a London committee of the Women's Social and Political Union. A permanent London organisation.

Annie You could go to London when you finish your law studies.

Christabel *You* could go now.

Annie Me?

Christabel Do you think you could rouse London to militant action?

Annie I don't see why not. I'll need some money.

Christabel How much? How much money to rouse London?

Annie (*Casual, but meaning it*) Two pounds should be enough.

Scene: **Sylvia's studio.** *It is part sitting-room and, in the near future, will become part headquarters of the London committee. It has a built-in discipline, even austerity, that prevents it being a mere shambles. There are paintings on the wall and an unfinished canvas on an easel.* **Annie** *and* **Sylvia** *come in, each carrying a suitcase. They put the cases down and* **Annie** *looks at the room, eager to be impressed.*

Sylvia (*Referring to the cases*) Is this all?

Annie All my worldly goods.

Sylvia A lot of people have much less.

(*Their relationship is quiet and tentative, unlike the instant chemistry that exists between* **Annie** *and* **Christabel.** *There is a knock at the door*)

Sylvia Sit down. Make yourself at home.

Annie Had a long sit in the train . . . I'll wander a bit if that's all right. . . . (*She wanders about, inspecting* **Sylvia's** *paintings*) Are these all yours?

Sylvia Yes.

Annie They're beautiful.

Sylvia They should be better.

Annie No, really . . . they're lovely.

Sylvia Thank you. (*Pause*) I don't work hard enough.

Annie You never stop working, according to your mother.

Sylvia I don't work hard enough at the painting. Always in trouble at the college. Give up political work, concentrate on your studies. But I take no notice.

Annie It's the same with Christabel. (*She sits down*) She's a marvellous person, Christabel.

Sylvia So everybody tells me.

(**Annie** *reacts quickly to* **Sylvia's** *dry comment*)

Annie They say you're marvellous, too.

Sylvia (*Half-smile*) And you've acquired a reputation for quick thinking. I see why.

Annie I'm going to see Keir Hardie tomorrow.

Sylvia There's a well-worn path from here to Keir Hardie's....

Annie I thought there might be.

Sylvia And when you've had a day to settle in, I'll show you some of the sights....

Annie I'd like to go to the National Gallery....

Sylvia Not those sights. I mean the sights they don't talk about in polite circles ... the East End. Have a look at some East End faces, that's the real National Gallery....

(**Sylvia** *is very serious and earnest again: her true role.* **Annie's** *eyes wander again towards the paintings. She focuses on one in particular. It is an East End scene*)

Scene: **Keir Hardie's flat. Keir Hardie** *and* **Annie** *are in friendly conference: they are old friends.*

Hardie I know you worship the ground that Christabel Pankhurst walks on ... no doubt with good reason. But Sylvia's sowing the seeds where they'll bring forth the fruit your movement needs.

Annie In the East End?

Hardie Among the working classes. It'll be their support that'll win the day for you in the end.

Annie I brought my clogs and shawl with me.

Hardie Did you now?

Annie I take them everywhere.

Hardie I thought you were resolved never to wear those again.

Annie We thought ... if we march on Downing Street ... or lobby Parliament, anything like that ... the clogs and shawl look more interesting on photographs. In the newspapers. They attract attention, especially in London. That's what we think, anyway.

Hardie That's what Christabel thinks.

Annie It might have been her idea ... I don't have many ideas of my own.

Hardie Annie, my love. Just a wee warning.

Annie What about?

Hardie Especially now you're in London. Don't let anybody patronise you.

Annie Who's likely to do that?

Hardie Anybody. Believe me, Annie, I *know*. Any son or daughter of the working class who shows the brain and the intelligence to move among the Lords and Masters . . . like you . . . and like me . . . give the Lords and Masters half a chance, they'll turn you into a performing monkey. I see it in my own party. The new Labour members. They enjoy the patronage, the wining and dining . . . and it destroys them in the end. They don't even know it's happening. (*Pause*) Don't let other people pull the strings, Annie. Keep tight hold of the strings. That way, you'll keep tight hold of your own soul.

Annie I'll do my best.

Hardie Aye. I'll back you to survive. Now let's do some work.

Annie That's what I'm here for.

Hardie Have you heard of Mr and Mrs Pethick Lawrence?

Annie I've heard a little about them.

Hardie They're good organisers. That's the other thing you need . . . organisation . . . to go with your working-class support. You'll get organisation from Frederick and Emmeline . . . if you can persuade them to co-operate. . . .

Annie I'll persuade them.

Hardie I give you fair warning. Mrs Pankhurst tried to get them involved but they refused . . . said they were already too busy, too many commitments . . . which happens to be true. So you'll have to work a wee bit.

Annie (*Totally confident*) It'll be all right.

Hardie Now, if there's anything else. . . .

Annie Yes. One thing.

Hardie (*Anticipating her*) I know, I'll tell you which bus to catch. (*He is very warm and paternal*) Get on the first bus that comes along, mention my name to the driver and tell him where you want to go . . . you'll have no trouble.

Scene: **The Pethick Lawrence apartment. Frederick** *and* **Emmeline** *greet* **Annie**.

Butler Miss Annie Kenney.

Frederick (*To* **Butler**) Thank you. (*He shakes hands with* **Annie** *as the* **Butler** *goes out*) Hello, Miss Kenney.

Annie Hello, Mr Pethick Lawrence.

Frederick My wife, Emmeline. . . .

Emmeline I'm delighted to meet you, Miss Kenney. . . .

Annie I'm delighted too.

Frederick Do sit down (*They sit down*) Have you fully recovered from your experiences in prison?

Annie Prison? Oh yes. I'd forgotten about prison, it was so long ago.

Frederick Good. Now please don't think me rude, Miss Kenney, but before you tell us why you've come here . . . and we're both well enough informed to guess why you've come . . . I must ask you to be reasonably brief as we both have other meetings to attend. . . .

Annie I want you to join our movement . . . the woman's suffrage movement.

Emmeline What sort of help would you need?

Annie Mr Keir Hardie suggested you'd be the ideal person to be the first National Treasurer of the Women's Social and Political Union.

(*This is rather more than* **Emmeline** *expected*)

Emmeline The National Treasurer?

Annie The first. He said you were efficient and business-like. We're not efficient and business-like. They won't even answer our questions. We end up in prison.

Frederick Have you any funds?

Annie Not really. They gave me two pounds to come to London with, but that's nearly gone. I think we're probably in debt.

Frederick Honorary Treasurer, with the emphasis on 'Honorary'. . . .

Annie Part of the idea is that the Honorary Treasurer would raise funds for the campaign. It's all been Mrs Pankhurst's own money so far, and she's not a rich woman. She's as poor as me, though she doesn't admit it. Mr Keir Hardie said you'd be good at raising money.

Emmeline What a talkative man he is.

Annie I'm sure Sylvia would donate a painting.

Frederick A painting?

Annie If you decided to hold a raffle. Am I talking too much? I don't want to delay you. I mean, these are details of policy, really. . . .

Emmeline I hope you don't want an immediate answer.

Annie Of course not, I don't like to rush anybody. . . .

Frederick And I'm sure Mr Keir Hardie must have said . . . give them time, let the idea simmer. . . .

Annie Yes. He said something like that. He's a marvellous man.

Emmeline And so eloquent.

Frederick Very.

(*This is a private joke between them*)

Emmeline How much time will you allow me? To simmer?

Annie We're having a meeting tomorrow night. At Sylvia's . . . that's where I'm staying . . . 45, Park Walk, Chelsea . . . at seven-thirty. . . . If you could come along, meet Sylvia and the others . . . hear all about our campaign . . . (*Pause*) You *will* come, won't you?

(*A pause during which* **Frederick** *and* **Emmeline** *exchange glances*)

Emmeline No promises.

Annie I didn't come for promises . . . just say you'll come to the meeting. . . .

Emmeline All right.

Annie (*She stands up*) I'll be quiet now, so you can go to your meetings. Sylvia's taking me to the East End to further my education . . . there's a lot to know, isn't there?

Frederick Yes. Quite a lot.

Annie But it's all exciting.

Scene: **Sylvia's studio.** *The room is set for a committee meeting. Around the table are eight people:* **Sylvia, Annie, Emmeline Pethick Lawrence, Mrs Roe,** *the landlady, plus* **Mrs Clarke, Mary Neal, Mrs Fenwick Miller** *and* **Mrs Martell:** *none of these last four speaks during the scene.* **Sylvia** *is acting as chairman of the meeting.*

Sylvia The resolution is that the Central London Committee of the Women's Social and Political Union be formed. . . . (*She looks for a show of hands: all hands go up*) Unanimously. (*She notes this in the minutes – she's acting as secretary, too*) Next. The post of Honorary Secretary.

Annie I propose Sylvia.

Mrs Roe Seconded.

Sylvia Are there any other nominations?

(*There are none*)

Annie I think you'd better write 'Unanimously'.

(**Sylvia** *looks at them: all hands go up*)

Sylvia Thank you all very much. I'll do my best. (*There is a pause while she makes the note in the minutes*) Next. The position of National Treasurer.

Annie I propose Mrs Pethick Lawrence.

Mrs Roe Seconded.

Emmeline Perhaps Mrs Pethick Lawrence isn't prepared to accept the nomination....

Sylvia If there are any questions we can answer to help make up your mind....

Emmeline Well, I know you have no money.

Sylvia Correct.

Emmeline Do you have any place in mind as an office? A headquarters?

Sylvia We thought here....

Mrs Roe You're all most welcome.

Emmeline What about your studies?

Sylvia I'll....

Mrs Roe (*Breaking in*) She'll do that through the night, same as she does at the moment....

Emmeline What about the rest of the London organisation?

Sylvia We *are* the London organisation.

Emmeline I see. (*Pause*) Any ... assets? Stationery? Stamps? A typewriter?

Annie (*Sudden thought*) Flora Drummond might get us a typewriter. She works for the Oliver company in Manchester....

Sylvia But I think you'll be starting with a totally clean sheet, Mrs Pethick Lawrence. (*She smiles.* **Emmeline** *hesitates*)

Emmeline I'll accept the nomination.

Annie I think it will be carried unanimously.

Emmeline I shouldn't be surprised.

(*It is unanimous*)

(*Interval, if wanted*)

Scene: **Sylvia's studio. Sylvia** *and* **Annie,** *alone after their meeting, are drinking their late-night cocoa.*

Annie I did enjoy this evening.

Sylvia The meeting.

Annie Yes. I really think we're getting somewhere. You know . . . if anybody told me . . . a year ago . . . the way things were going to happen . . . being in London, meeting people like the Pethick Lawrences. . . .

Sylvia People like the Pethick Lawrences?

Annie Yes. . . .(*She is puzzled by the challenge in* **Sylvia's** *voice*) They are rather special, aren't they?

Sylvia They've got money *and* a social conscience. It's an unusual combination.

Annie It's not *their* fault they've got money. . . .

Sylvia No. It's ours. Your fault and my fault.

Annie I'm sorry, I . . . don't understand.

Sylvia (*Breaking in*) Annie. You're happier than you were a year ago. You find fulfilment in the work.

Annie Of course.

Sylvia But you mustn't make the mistake of thinking it's for your benefit. I'm not important and you're not important. It's the mistake that Christabel makes.

Annie Christabel?

Sylvia The lovely lady Christabel. She's fighting for the emancipation of women . . . but the person she's really emancipating is herself. Watch her when she's making a speech . . . or watch her when she comes out of prison . . . you're watching an emancipated woman. . . . (*Pause*) But that's not the problem.

Annie Tell me.

Sylvia Watch the prison gates. When one of our people is released.

Scene: **The prison gates.** *Exactly as before, when the reception committee met* **Annie. Teresa Billington, Jessie Kenney** *and* **Mrs Pankhurst** *stand outside the gates. There are at least two bouquets of flowers and a waiting taxi. One of the other released women glances back to see what the fuss is about before she shuffles on. Against these images, we hear* **Sylvia's** *voice.*

Sylvia You see a reception committee . . . flowers . . . kisses and applause and smiles for the world. A taxi to take you to a hearty breakfast and an interview with the press. But watch the other women. The ones who slink away silently . . . no flowers, no kisses, no taxis, probably no breakfast either . . . they're the ones, Annie. . . .

Scene: **Sylvia's studio.** *This is a continuation of the earlier scene.* **Annie** *and* **Sylvia** *are as they were.*

Sylvia The battle's for those women . . . not for us . . . we don't matter.

(*Pause*)

Annie Like . . . the women on the Thames Embankment?

Sylvia Yes.

Scene: **The Thames Embankment.** *A group of men and women is sleeping rough on the Embankment. One of the women is by any outward physical and social standards a tramp; it is difficult to be precise about her age because she's really timeless and universal. If she had a name, she lost it: we will call her* **Mary. Mary** *smiles at* **Annie:** *the teeth are irregular but the spirit is shining.*

Annie Would you like a cup of tea?

Scene: **A caff.** *'Caff' is an exact description of this establishment.* **Annie** *and* **Mary** *sit at a rough wooden table with large mugs of tea.*

Mary You're very kind, dear.

Annie Not really.

Mary They sometimes do this, you know, The well-dressed ladies . . . ladies of quality . . . they come down the Embankment and give us food or something to drink or new boots. . . . We watch for them coming . . . try to look cold and hungry as they walk past so's they'll notice us. . . . Oh, yes, ladies of quality, very refined. . . . (*Pause*) Not like you.

Annie I do my best.

Mary Oh, you've got quality, dear. But not born to it.

Annie I used to be a mill girl.

Mary From the North?

Annie Yes.

Mary I can tell. I've travelled a great deal, you see. Oh yes, you're one of us. You know what it's like . . . being shut in.

Annie Shut in? Yes, I know about that. I've been in prison.

Mary Prison? So you'll know about freedom as well.

Annie I've walked the Pennine hills. . . .

Mary Cathedrals I like.

Annie Did you say cathedrals?

Mary Surprises people, that. I've seen them all, well, mostly. Salisbury and Durham and Truro. . . .

Annie Walking?

Mary No money for fares. I take my own time. There's no hurry when you're a pilgrim. You know where you're going. You know it'll be there when you get there.

Annie Like the great city.

Mary That I couldn't say. I've always wanted to go to Russia. Now *there's* a pilgrimage for you. But I don't suppose I'll ever go. I stick to my cathedrals. They're always there. Twice as big as you expected. Twice as grand. They don't let you down.

(*Pause*)

Annie Do you believe in God?

Mary Not a lot, dear, to be honest. Don't be offended but. . . .

Annie I'm not.

Mary When you're lying there and you're cold and you're hungry, well, if you start believing in God you're bound to say he's not making a very good job of things. I might start believing in him when he makes a better job of running things. (*Pause*) No. I believe in my cathedrals, I believe in them, oh yes. (*Pause*) Always there, right where you expected them.

Scene: **Sylvia's studio.** *In effect this is a continuation of* **Annie's** *and* **Sylvia's** *conversation after the meeting.*

Sylvia For Christabel, the movement is her life.

Annie And your mother too?

Sylvia Her life as well. But that's not enough. For me, it has to be a sacrifice of my life.

Annie You're not like Christabel or your mother, are you?

Sylvia Different . . . but the same. Different ways of doing things . . . but the same passion. When I quarrel with my mother . . . you've never heard us quarrel have you? You can hear it for miles around . . . but we quarrel because we share the same passions . . . because we care. . . .

Annie But I don't understand the difference. . . .

Sylvia Simple. My mother . . . and Christabel too. They devote their life to the movement . . . they haven't sacrificed anything else. I have. If I was sent on this earth to do anything, it was to paint pictures. I may not be very good at it, you can't tell . . . but it's a hard job being a bad artist even. . . . It's what I really want to do, Annie, paint pictures. But when I look at the women on the Embankment . . . painting pictures seems like an obscenity. Just . . . not important. . . . Only to me is it important. And that's not good enough.

Scene: **Keir Hardie's flat. Hardie** *sits reading through his papers. There is a sharp, business-like knock on the door.*

Hardie Come in.

(**Annie** *comes in very briskly. The whole sequence should be busy and practical: a sharp contrast to the preceding scene*)

Annie Good morning.

Hardie Good morning, Annie. You're looking very pleased with yourself. . . .

Annie We've done it!

Hardie What have you done?

Annie We've booked the Caxton Hall for our first public meeting in London. February sixteenth. The day the new Liberal Government assembles . . . but it's *us* they'll be listening to. . . .

Hardie The Caxton Hall? It's a big hall, it'll take some filling. . . .

Annie We'll fill it.

Hardie As long as it's with people, not with hot air. . . .

Annie All Sylvia's working women from the East End, they'll be coming. . . .

Hardie Have you asked them?

Annie Not yet.

Hardie Somebody will have to pay their fares to get them there. . . .

Annie And we'll give them something to eat and drink when they arrive at the hall. . . .

Hardie Good girl, you're thinking ahead of me. . . .

Annie Except that what with that, and the hire of the hall, and cost of printing and. . . .

Hardie You're short of money.

Annie That's why I came to see you.

Hardie I was thinking it was pure and simple affection. . . .

Annie Well, of course it's that as well but . . . we really need another fifty pounds. The Pethick Lawrences have helped but we're still short. . . .

Hardie Are you looking for a loan or a gift?

Annie Honestly, we're not fussy . . . we're fully prepared to accept either. . . .

Hardie The nobility shines like a beacon. . . .

Annie I beg your pardon?

(*Pause*)

Hardie There's W. T. Stead . . . he might be prepared to help . . . and Isabel Ford. . . . Mind you, I've got about a dozen schemes of my own that I'm trying to enlist their support for. . . .

Annie If you give me their addresses. . . . (*Hesitates*)

Hardie Yes?

Annie I'll race you to them.

Hardie I wouldn't even enter a race against you, Annie Kenney. . . .

Scene: **Sylvia's studio**. *The door flies open and Annie comes in, very pleased with herself.*

Annie I got the money! (*She pauses and does a kind of double take. In the room, apart from* **Sylvia,** *are* **Teresa Billington** *and* **Jessie Kenney**) Jessie! Tess!

Teresa We thought you might need a little help. . . .

Annie Oh, we do . . . no question, we need some help. . . .

(*She crosses to them and they embrace* **Annie** *in turn*)

Jessie How are you, Annie?

Annie I'm fine.

Jessie You look exhausted, but you always did.

Annie (*To* **Teresa**) How long are you staying in London?

Teresa Permanently, I hope.

Annie That's marvellous.

Sylvia How much money did you get, Annie?

Annie Two twenty-five-pound loans . . . but they might turn into very long-term loans. . . . Do you think we might buy a typewriter? (*She turns to* **Jessie**) We want to circulate every Member of Parliament.

(*All this time* **Sylvia** *is quietly sketching on a drawing pad.* **Annie** *crosses to her to have a look*)

Annie That's lovely, Sylvia. . . . (*To the others*) Sylvia's designing our banner for the meeting. . . . (*To* **Sylvia**) Did you get any chalks?

Sylvia On the table.

(*On the table is a box of chalks.* **Annie** *picks up the box*)

Sylvia Courtesy of the art college.

Scene: **A street.** *It is in a working-class neighbourhood of the East End.* **Annie** *is on her hands and knees chalking on the pavement. It is tedious and uncomfortable work. She writes:* 'WSPU Public Meeting. Caxton Hall. Main Speaker: Mrs Pankhurst. Votes for Women!' *She adds artistic touches – multi-coloured underlinings, shadowing the letters and so on. She rubs her knees as she stands up to inspect her work.*

Scene: **Keir Hardie's flat. Hardie** *and* **Sylvia** *are talking.*

Sylvia So we wondered whether we might have the occasional use of this place for the next few days. . . .

Hardie As long as you don't expect me to prepare meals for you.

Sylvia We might even prepare an occasional meal for you. . . .

Hardie That's very gracious, Sylvia, I accept your offer.

Sylvia A token of our admiration and affection. . . .

Hardie And what's the ulterior motive?

Sylvia You've got a telephone. We haven't.

(*They smile, because it's the easy teasing of old comrades*)

Scene: **Sylvia's studio. Annie** *and* **Teresa** *are in the foreground –* **Annie** *still with her street-chalking working clothes on.*

Annie How many loaves will we need?

Teresa How many women are coming?

Annie We won't really know until the night. . . .

Teresa You'd better order five loaves and two fishes. . . .

Jessie And leave the rest to Mrs Pankhurst. . . .

Flora The Gospel according to St Matthew says it was seven loaves.

Annie I'm going to order one hundred.

Teresa Can we afford it?

Annie I'll open an account somewhere. I've learned *that* much about London.

Scene: **Keir Hardie's flat. Sylvia** *is alone: on the telephone.*

Sylvia Hello? Is that *The Times*? I'd like to speak to the editor please. . . . (*She waits, then speaks as the* **Editor** *materialises at the other end*) Good afternoon, this is Sylvia Pankhurst of the Women's Social and Political Union. Did you receive our letter about the Caxton Hall meeting?

Scene: **An East End street. Annie** *is struggling with a huge poster advertising a meeting. She is attempting to stick it to a bare brick wall.*

Scene: **Sylvia's studio.** *In contrast to the last time we were here, this is a quiet, wee-small-hours scene.* **Annie** *is asleep in a chair by the fire.* **Sylvia** *is painting a banner – which she has fixed so that it covers most of one wall of the studio.* **Teresa** *comes in with a tray carrying three cups of cocoa.*

Teresa She's asleep.

Sylvia Yes. (*Pause*) She was chattering away, sixteen to the dozen, then suddenly it stopped.

Teresa I won't wake her. (*She puts the tray down and takes a drink to* **Sylvia**) There.

Sylvia Thank you, Tess.

Teresa Do you know what time it is?

Sylvia No.

Teresa Twenty past two.

Sylvia I always work well after midnight. As my ladies would say . . . (*She goes into a Cockney accent*) focuses the mind somefink remarkable.

Teresa Yes, but. . . . (*She hesitates*) You could do yourself permanent damage.

Sylvia I've already done that. So it's no longer a problem.

Scene: **Keir Hardie's flat.** *Now it's* **Annie** *on the telephone.*

Annie Yes . . . one hundred loaves to be delivered to the Caxton Hall tomorrow night . . . by five o'clock? That's very good. . . . (*The caller at the other end of the phone is about to hang up but* **Annie** *calls him back*) There's just one more thing. . . . You don't happen to know where we can borrow a tea urn . . . well, not one, more like a dozen, I suppose. . . . Thank you, we've already tried the Salvation Army. . . .

Scene: **Sylvia's studio.** *The banner is about to be 'unveiled': of course* **Sylvia** *would not dream of such a theatrical gesture as a physical unveiling. She just stands aside.*

Sylvia I'll have to call that finished.

(**Annie**, **Jessie** *and* **Teresa** *all stop whatever they are doing to look*)

Sylvia I've had to rush it too much, but. . . .

Annie If you want a job doing, you ask a busy person. . . .

Jessie What our mother always said.

Teresa She was right. It's absolutely splendid.

(*They are standing in a group admiring* **Sylvia's** *work – and by implication their own – when the door opens and* **Mrs Pankhurst** *walks in*)

Mrs Pankhurst So this is the mad-house. . . .

Sylvia I beg your pardon, mother?

Mrs Pankhurst The lunatic asylum.

Sylvia What are you talking about?

Mrs Pankhurst I'm talking about sensible, grown women who are sent to London to organise political action and in a matter of two or three weeks you book the largest hall you can get your hands on, heaven knows at what cost to the movement . . . and I find myself committed to addressing a meeting that will be attended by rows and rows of empty seats. Is it too late to cancel it?

Sylvia Much too late, yes.

Mrs Pankhurst It will set back the cause several years. Just imagine what the press will say . . . last night Mrs Pankhurst addressed a meeting in London . . . the first London rally of the Women's Social and Political Union . . . she received a lukewarm reception from an audience of twenty-five, most of them friends of the family . . .

Sylvia That's not fair.

Mrs Pankhurst I was making speeches before you were born. You develop instincts for these things. . . .

(*There is a rather uneasy silence.* **Annie** *leaps in*)

Annie You're wrong, Mrs Pankhurst. The hall will be full. Packed to overflowing.

Mrs Pankhurst Who will this splendid audience consist of?

Annie Our supporters from the East End.

Mrs Pankhurst How many? Ten? Twenty?

Annie We think about four hundred. We're paying their fares and we're feeding them when they arrive at the hall.

Mrs Pankhurst If this were Oldham or Manchester, I would believe you. As it is, I can only hope and pray that you are right. (*She goes to the door*) I'll see what I can do to rescue the movement from this disaster.

(*She sweeps out. There is another uneasy silence.* **Sylvia** *looks across at* **Annie**)

Sylvia Thank you.

Annie I hope I wasn't rude.

Sylvia It's very hard to insult my mother. It might do her good if more people tried. . . .

Annie (*Crossing over to* **Sylvia**) It's a lovely banner.

Sylvia Good. (*Pause*) Annie. I *do* hope you're right.

Annie (*Revealing for the first time* her *secret fears about the meeting*) Sylvia. So do I.

Scene: **Caxton Hall.** *The rows of empty seats suggest at first that the worst fears have been realised. Then, at the back of the hall, we find a group, including* **Annie, Jessie** *and* **Teresa,** *working at a trestle table preparing food.* **Annie** *is hard at work slicing bread while* **Jessie** *and* **Teresa** *are buttering.*

Annie Do you think I ordered too much? (*She pauses between loaves to exercise her aching wrists*)

Jessie All we can do is wait and see.

Teresa Say a quick prayer. That might help.

Annie I was sure everything would be all right until Mrs Pankhurst. . . . (*She is interrupted by a shout from* **Sylvia** *off stage*)

Sylvia Is that all right? (*She comes onto the stage and arranges a banner behind the table which is set for the platform party. She has made a good and colourful job of the platform*)

Teresa (*Shouts*) It looks marvellous.

Jessie (*Quietly*) I hope somebody's here to see it.

Teresa I'm waiting to hear Mrs Pankhurst apologise.

Annie Whatever for?

Jessie You know what for.

Teresa She had no right to say those things to you and Sylvia. . . .

Annie Whether there's five people or five hundred, all Mrs Pankhurst has to do is make a speech. That's all. Nothing more. (**Annie** *doesn't bear grudges*)

Teresa You've got to make a speech, too, don't forget.

Annie I prefer cutting bread. (**Teresa** *pushes another loaf towards* **Annie**)

Teresa Thank you. (*As* **Annie** *cuts another loaf she quietly practises her speech*)

Annie 'Madam Chairman, ladies, sisters . . . this is the first public meeting to be held in London. . . .' (**Sylvia** *enters*)

Sylvia Annie, you've won! (*She opens the doors and* **Women** *enter in a mass.* **Annie** *sighs a deep sigh of relief and closes her eyes briefly.* **Annie** *mounts the stage to make her speech. The audience is mainly composed of working-class women with a sprinkling of middle-class ladies wearing, in some cases, their servants' clothes in a vain effort not to look conspicuous. The East End contingent has red Labour Party banners but these are furled up and concealed at this point. On the platform we see all our principals:* **Mrs Pankhurst, Sylvia, Christabel, Teresa, Emmeline, Jessie** *and behind them, the banner*)

Annie Madam Chairman, ladies . . . sisters. . . . This is the first public meeting to be held in London by the Women's Social and Political Union. That may sound to you like a lot of big words . . . and so they are to me, because I had to practise that bit several times before the meeting to be sure of getting it right. (*Ripple of laughter*) I won't use any more big words. I'll leave that to those who are cleverer than me . . . which means practically everybody. I'm just going to tell you what this movement means to me. It all started, believe it or not, because I sang in a choir . . . which is very silly because I can't even sing. (*Laughter*) I used to open my mouth in time with the others, and hope that nobody would notice there was no noise. It was through the choir that I met the Pankhursts . . . and through them my life changed. When I try to explain how my life has changed, I keep thinking of one of the songs we used to sing. I won't sing it now but I will tell you some of the words . . . like this it goes. . . .

'From street and square, from hill and glen,
Of this vast world beyond my door,
I hear the tread of marching men,
The patient armies of the poor.

'Not ermine-clad or clothed in state,
Their title-deeds not yet made plain,
But waking early, toiling late,
The heirs of all the earth remain.'

And it finishes. . . .

'Some day, without a trumpet call,
The news will o'er the world be blown,
The heritage comes back to all;
The myriad monarchs take their own.'

I am one of the patient armies of the poor. And so are most of you. But we're not content to be patient any longer. (*There are cries of:* 'Hear. Hear.') It is time to take back our heritage. It is time to take back our own. I believe . . . we believe . . . that the first step must be the vote. We all know the ancient cry: No taxation without representation. I think it's time to alter that. We should say: No exploitation without representation. No slums without representation. . . . And when the day comes that we – the women of Great Britain – have representation . . . I predict that in a strange and miraculous way, we will look and we will see that these other things have vanished . . . the exploitation and the slums and the starvation. . . . At the very least, we can't make a worse mess than our gentlemen politicians . . . and at the very best, we shall walk equally with men, and with them take possession of our true heritage. (*Applause*) My sisters . . . I thank you for listening to me. Now it is my great honour and privilege to introduce our very special guest speaker . . . beloved of all Prime Ministers . . . beloved of all of us here in this hall: Mrs Pankhurst. . . .

(**Mrs Pankhurst** *stands up and crosses to* **Annie.** *There is loud and enthusiastic applause for both of them.* **Annie** *is about to return to her seat but* **Mrs Pankhurst** *takes her hand and forces her to acknowledge the applause*)

Mrs Pankhurst Annie. . . . I apologise.

Annie There's nothing to apologise for. . . .

Mrs Pankhurst Oh me of little faith.

Annie Listen. . . .

(*They turn again towards the audience. The* **Women** *are standing, Labour Party banners are displayed and we hear, without identifying the singer, a* **Woman** *singing the opening lines of* The Red Flag. *The singing swells to a mighty chorus. The platform party join in and the audience sway their banners*)

All 'The workers' flag is deepest red,
It shrouded oft our martyred dead.

And ere their limbs grew stiff and cold
Their life-blood dyed its every fold.
Then raise the scarlet banner high,
Beneath its fold we'll live and die.
Though cowards flinch and traitors sneer,
We'll keep the red flag flying here.'

(*As the song ends the applause and cheering builds and then dies away in a sudden long echo. The hall is now deserted and* **Annie** *sits alone.* **Sylvia** *and* **Flora** *come on to the platform and start removing the decorations. Their voices murmur.* **Teresa** *walks past* **Annie**)

Teresa Look. (**Annie** *looks.* **Teresa** *holds up a five-pound note to show her*) Five pounds. Donation from Lady Carlisle.

Annie Good.

Teresa That's nearly fifty pounds in donations and promises. . . .

Annie Good.

(**Teresa** *walks on to tell somebody else the good news.* **Mrs Pankhurst** *is with a group of* **Women** *across the hall.* **Annie's** *eyes move briefly in her direction*)

Mrs Pankhurst We're lobbying Parliament tomorrow . . . and there's a very good chance Campbell Bannerman will receive a deputation in the very near future. . . .

(**Mrs Pankhurst's** *voice fades as* **Christabel** *approaches* **Annie.** *She sits down in a seat near* **Annie**)

Christabel Tired?

Annie Five minutes . . . to get my breath back.

Christabel Don't worry. It really happened.

Annie My mother used to say: You don't know your own strength until you try.

Christabel Even got money to pay some of the bills.

(*Pause.* **Christabel** *takes out her notebook*)

Annie Still the notebook?

Christabel There's more to write down. More every day.

Annie Yes.

Christabel It says here . . . London.

Annie Well done, Christabel. This *is* London.

Christabel In the summer . . . when I finish my law studies . . . mother's going to sell up in Manchester. We're moving down here.

Annie The heart of the Empire.

Christabel Our Empire. (*Pause*) And it says here . . . 'Singing'. . . . (*She refers to her notebook*)

Annie Funny thing to write down.

Christabel You said in your speech tonight . . . you can't sing.

Annie I can't.

Christabel You can sing, Annie. Tonight you did.

(*Pause*)

Annie Well . . . I thought, once or twice, just the odd sentence in the speech . . . I thought it was me talking and not somebody else. That makes a change.

Christabel You sang. (*Pause*) Lobbying Parliament tomorrow.

Annie Yes. (*Brief Pause*) Tonight the song. Tomorrow . . . Westminster. The day after . . . the great city. (*She looks at her hands*) Look, all chalk and breadcrumbs.

(*They are the last two in the hall. Slowly they make their way out.* **Annie** *pausing here and there to pick up a discarded poster or such. We hear the* **Choir** *singing over their departure*)

Choir 'Some day, without a trumpet call,
The news will o'er the world be blown,
The heritage comes back to all;
The myriad monarchs take their own.'

(*The music fades. Somebody switches the lights out. Darkness*)

The End

ACTIVITIES

Lady Constance Lytton, Annie Kenny, Emmeline Pethick Lawrence, Christabel Pankhurst, Sylvia Pankhurst.

Arrest of a militant Suffragette.

Annie Kenney on Stage

Putting a television play like *Annie Kenney* on stage presents special difficulties since it requires a large number of scenes and a variety of indoor and outdoor locations. These problems can be overcome by using a stylised presentation.

This might include:

- the use of slides or acetates on an overhead projector to establish scenes
- sound effects as a substitute for scenery (e.g. at the fairground)
- hand-held props (the use of stage scenery would restrict the pace and flow of the performance)
- lighting changes as a substitute for the cuts used in the television production.

All of these ideas could be presented in theatre in the round and on an almost empty stage. Period costumes would play an important part in establishing the historical context.

The following is a list of scenes that would be needed.

Rooms

The Kenneys' living room (one scene)
The Pankhurst's living room at Nelson Street (three scenes)
The prison visitors' room (two scenes)
Sylvia's studio (nine scenes)
Keir Hardie's flat (five scenes)
The Pethick Lawrence apartment (one scene)

Public places

The Co-Op Hall (two scenes)
The Free Trade Hall (one scene)
A magistrates' court (one scene)
Caxton Hall (one scene)
A caff (one scene)

Exteriors

A Pennine valley (two scenes)
A fairground (one scene)
Outside the prison (two scenes)
A park (one scene)
The Thames Embankment (one scene)
East End Streets (two scenes)

1 In a group, imagine you are a theatre production company who wish to stage *Annie Kenney*. You want the production to take place at the Open Space Theatre. The diagram shows the layout of this theatre. Unfortunately there are several other groups who wish to stage the play and it will be necessary to present your production plans to the Open Space Management Committee who will have to decide which is likely to be the most effective production.

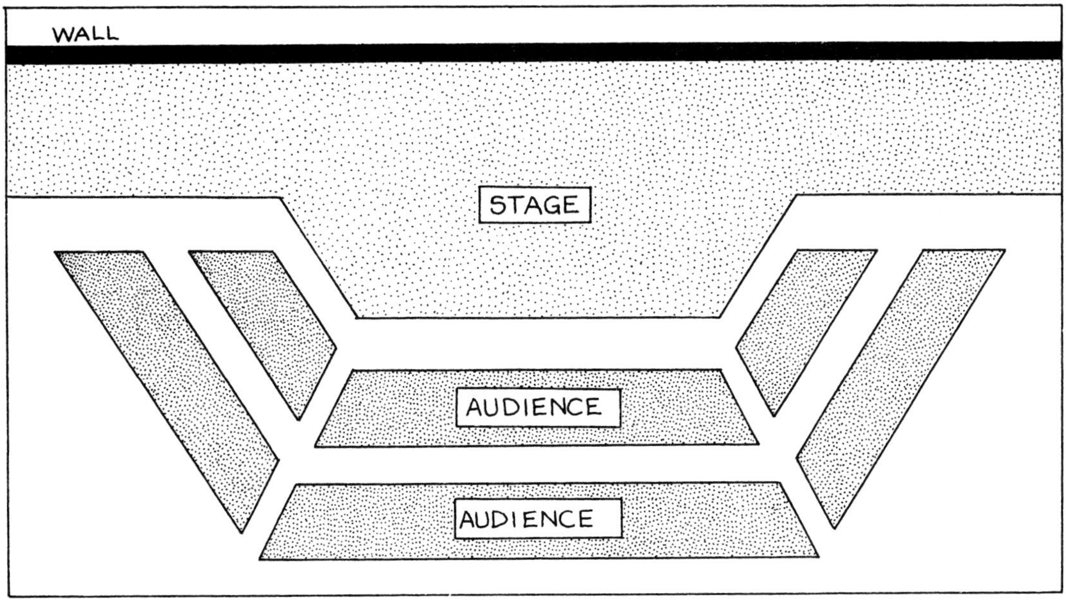

Divide the different aspects of your production between members of the group and prepare an oral presentation. Your presentation will involve showing the committee your work and explaining the thinking behind the decisions you have made. Each group will elect one person to sit on the management committee.

Areas to cover are listed below.

- Cast the play using well-known stars.
- Design the costumes for at least three characters in the play, *or* design three different costumes which Annie Kenney would wear for different scenes in the play.
- Choose three scenes from the play and design the stage for them. You should decide on any backdrop image, and on a copy of the stage plan mark entrances, exits, scenery and props.
- Prepare a lighting plan which gives brief notes about the lighting effects for each scene.
- Present your plans for the programme. Historical notes may be helpful for the audience. You will find some useful data on pages 44–53.
- Prepare the publicity plans for your production. This could include posters, a trailer for local radio, advertisements in local newspapers.

Storyboard

A storyboard is a way of putting together words, pictures and sounds to plan a film or video sequence.

The following terms abbreviations are often used on storyboards:

SFX	sound effects	XCU	extreme close up
LS	long shot	Zoom in	gradually move closer to the subject
MS	medium shot	Zoom out	gradually move away from the subject
CU	close up	Pan	camera moves across a scene.

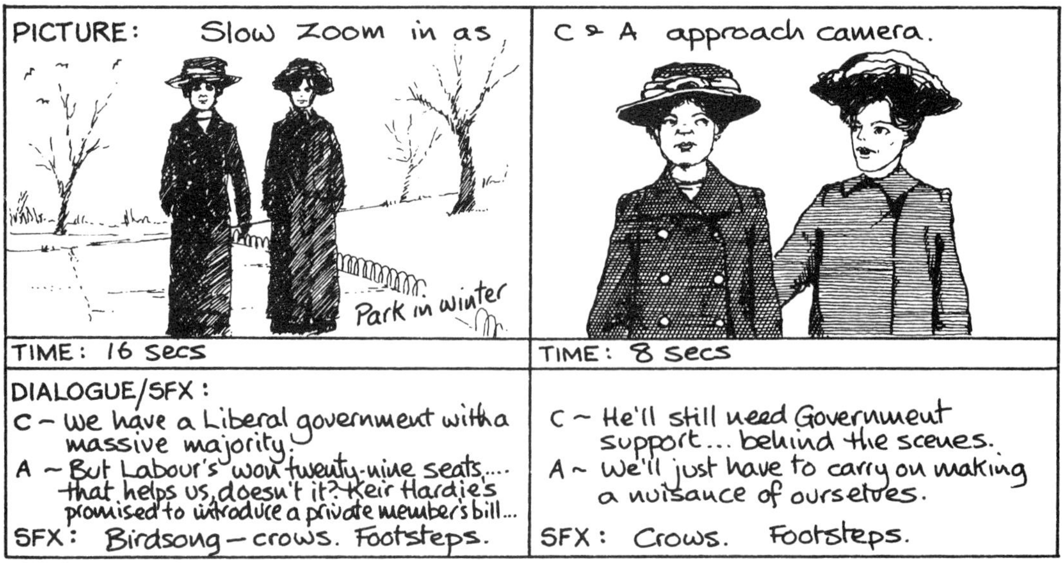

PICTURE: Slow zoom in as
C & A approach camera.
Park in winter
TIME: 16 secs
TIME: 8 secs
DIALOGUE/SFX:
C ~ We have a Liberal government with a massive majority.
A ~ But Labour's won twenty-nine seats.... that helps us, doesn't it? Keir Hardie's promised to introduce a private member's bill...
SFX: Birdsong – crows. Footsteps.
C ~ He'll still need Government support... behind the scenes.
A ~ We'll just have to carry on making a nuisance of ourselves.
SFX: Crows. Footsteps.

CU Christabel
MS
TIME: 3 secs
TIME: 8 secs
C ~ Is that enough, Annie?
SFX: Wind in trees
(C. takes out notebook)
A ~ What are you writing?
C ~ We must attack the problem at its heart. It is necessary to form a London Committee.
SFX: crows

Study the storyboard.

1 What mood do you think the scene conveys?

What emphasis is being given to the scene by the shots and sounds used?

2 *Either*

Write a new storyboard for this scene changing its emphasis and mood. Explain the changes you have made.

Or

Choose another scene from the play and storyboard it. Give brief notes to explain the effects you are trying to achieve.

PICTURE: MS
TIME: 10 secs
DIALOGUE/SFX:
A ~ You could go to London when you finish your law studies.
C ~ You could go now.
SFX: Swish of skirts
CU Annie
TIME: 5 secs
A ~ Me?
C ~ Do you think you could rouse London to militant action?
SFX: wind in trees
CU Annie
TIME: 8 secs
A ~ I don't see why not. I'll need some money.
C ~ How much? How much money to rouse London?
SFX: crows
MS
TIME: 5 secs
A ~ Two pounds should be enough.
Cut.
SFX: Footsteps. Swish of skirts.

Annie Kenney – Leader or Follower?

'She was essentially a follower . . . Her lack of perspective, her very intellectual limitations, lent her a certain directness of purpose when she became the instrument of a more powerful mind.'

Sylvia Pankhurst, *The Suffragette Movement*, 1931

1 Study the quotations below.

Annie I don't have many ideas. Mostly I remember other people's.

Annie Me? I'm not frightened of anybody.

Annie I don't know what I'd do if there weren't people around me, telling me what to think.

Christabel Do you think you can rouse London to militant action?
Annie I don't see why not.

Sylvia (to Annie) And you've acquired a reputation for quick thinking.

Annie ... That's what we think, anyway.
Hardie That's what Christabel thinks.
Annie It might have been her idea. I don't have many ideas of my own.

Annie ... I won't use any more big words. I'll leave that to those who are cleverer than me ... which is practically everybody.

Annie Well ... I thought once or twice, just the odd sentence in the speech ... I thought it was me talking and not somebody else. That makes a change.

2 Which scenes do the above quotations come from?

3 In groups discuss whether you agree with Sylvia Pankhurst's view that Annie Kenney was 'essentially a follower'. Use both the evidence presented here and your knowledge of the play to back up your opinions. What view do you think Annie had of herself?

4 Annie Kenney died in 1953. Write *two* obituaries for her. One for *The Times* and one for a magazine called *Rights for Women*. In your writing try to assess Annie Kenney's character and contribution to the beginning of the Suffragette movement. (It would be a good idea to look at some obituaries in the newspapers in your library.)

Relationships

Annie and Christabel

'Miss Pankhurst was more hesitating, more nervous than Miss Billington. She impressed me though. When the meeting was over, those in the audience whose minds responded more to cold logic drifted towards Teresa Billington; those who responded towards the human side drifted towards Miss Pankhurst. It was like a table where two courses were being served, one hot, the other cold. I found myself plate in hand where the hot course was being served. Before I knew what I had done I had promised to work up a meeting for Miss Pankhurst among thc factory women of Oldham and Leeds. I walked to the station with her and before we separated she asked me to spend the following Saturday afternoon with them at their home in Nelson Street.'

Annie Kenney's autobiography, *Memoirs of a Militant*, 1924

Later in her autobiography Annie Kenney says:

'I had faith in Christabel. It was exactly the faith of a child.'

1a Compare Annie Kenney's own account of her first meeting with Christabel with the version given in the play on pages 2–5. Do you think Alan Plater has reflected the emotions expressed by Annie? Which version reflects the power of Christabel's personality most strongly?

1b Write a further section of Annie's autobiography in which she comments on the impact of Christabel Pankhurst on her life and assesses her character.

Sylvia and Christabel

Look again at pages 22–3 and pages 24–5 in which Annie and Sylvia discuss commitment to the Suffragette cause.

2 In pairs improvise a discussion between Christabel and Sylvia which takes place shortly after the end of the play. Sylvia should try to persuade Christabel to give up her legal studies immediately rather than wait until the summer. Remember that these women are sisters.

Sylvia Pankhurst addressing a crowd in the East End.

The Language of Annie Kenney

1 In pairs, prepare a reading of the following scene between Annie Kenney and Mary, the woman from the Thames Embankment.

Before you begin consider:

- the 'tone' of the conversation
- the attitudes of the two characters towards each other
- the voices and accents you will need to use.

Scene: **A caff.** *'Caff' is an exact description of this establishment.* **Mary** *and* **Annie** *sit at a rough wooden table with large mugs of tea.*

Mary You're very kind, dear.
Annie Not really.
Mary They sometimes do this, you know, the well-dressed ladies ... ladies of quality ... they come down the Embankment and give us food or something to drink or new boots ... We watch them coming ... try to look cold and hungry as they walk past so's they'll notice us. Oh, yes, ladies of quality, very refined. ... (*Pause*) Not like you.
Annie I do my best.
Mary Oh you've got quality, dear, but not born to it.
Annie I used to be a mill girl.
Mary From the North?
Annie Yes.
Mary I can tell. I've travelled a great deal, you see. Oh yes, You're one of us. You know what it's like ... being shut in.
Annie Shut in? Yes, I know about that. I've been in prison.
Mary Prison? So you'll know about freedom as well.

When you have completed your paired reading discuss the following points in small groups.

2 Did anyone find it necessary to use a regional accent for their reading of either of the two characters? Why was this? What sort of accent did you use for Mary? What sort for Annie? Was there any point in the scene where you changed the accent used by Mary?

3 Look closely at the language used by Mary. How does it differ from the language used by Annie? Can you find an example of dialect used by Mary? Does Annie, a Lancashire mill girl, use dialect (see the page opposite if you are unsure about the difference between accent and dialect) in this passage? Does Annie use dialect at any other point in the play?

4 If you feel confident using accents prepare a second reading of the scene using different accents. For instance how would the scene work if Annie or Mary spoke with 'posh' accents? Would it be possible for Annie to use, for instance, an American accent?

Dialect means words and word orders used only in a particular area or by particular groups of people.

Accent means the way words are pronounced in a particular area or by particular groups of people.

Christabel Pankhurst in academic dress.

Annie Kenney in prison uniform.

Accent and Class

5 Study the following quotations from the play.

Christabel	Now ... we have been accused, not without reason, of being a middle-class organisation pursuing middle class aims
Annie	I'm speaking for the women who work in the mills ...
Bell	... If the evidence is true, the defendants have behaved like women from the slums. (**Annie** *is stung by this*)
Annie	I am a mill worker ... I went to the meeting ... as a representative of thousands of British working women ...
Annie	We thought ... if we march on Downing Street ... or lobby Parliament, anything like that ... the clogs and shawl look more interesting on photographs. In the newspapers. They attract attention especially in London.
Hardie	(To **Annie**) Any son or daughter of the working class ... like you... and like me ...
Annie	I am one of the patient armies of the poor.

It is clear that any production of *Annie Kenney* would need to show that Annie was working-class and one of the main ways this would be done would be through accent.

6 Imagine that your group is about to stage a production of *Annie Kenney*. Discuss what sort of accent you would wish the actress playing Annie to use.

7 Discuss why you think Alan Plater has chosen *not* to use dialect in Annie Kenney's speeches.

13 October 1905

1 Below is Christabel Pankhurst's description of the meeting at the Free Trade Hall which she disrupted with Annie Kenney. After you have read this account look back at pages 9–12 and compare the two versions of the events.

That night of the first arrest and imprisonment is unforgettable. The life of the Conservative Government was ebbing fast, so we wasted no powder and shot upon them. The Liberal leaders, who were to replace them in office, must be challenged on the fundamental principle of Liberalism – government of the people by the people, even such of the people as happened to be women. If the new Liberal Government were willing to enfranchise women, the Liberal leaders would say so; if they were not willing, then militancy would begin. A straight question must be put to them – a straight answer obtained.

Good seats were secured for the Free Trade Hall meeting. The question was painted on a banner in large letters, in case it should not be made clear enough by vocal utterance. How should we word it? 'Will you give woman suffrage?' – we rejected that form, for the word Suffrage suggested to some unlettered or jesting folk the idea of suffering. 'Let them suffer away' – we had heard the taunt. We must find another wording and we did! It was so obvious and yet, strange to say, quite new. Our banner bore this terse device:

WILL YOU GIVE
VOTES
FOR WOMEN?

Thus was uttered for the first time the famous and victorious battle-cry: 'Votes for Women!'

Busy with white calico, black furniture stain and paint-brushes, we soon had our banner ready, and Annie Kenney and I set forth to victory, in the form of an affirmative Liberal answer, or to prison. We knew only too well that the answer we longed for would be refused.

The Free Trade Hall was crowded. The sky was clear for a Liberal victory – save for a little cloud no bigger than a woman's hand! Calm, but within beating hearts, Annie and I took our seats and looked at the exultant throng we must soon anger by our challenge. Their cheers as the speakers entered gave us the note and pitch of their emotion. Speech followed speech. Interruptions came from eager partisans or from a few stray critics. The interrupters, we noticed, were ignored or good-humouredly answered. But, then, they were all men and voters! Our plan was to wait until the speakers had said their say, before asking our question. We must, for one thing, give these Liberal leaders and spokesmen the opportunity of explaining that their programme included political enfranchisement for women.

Annie as the working woman – for this should make the stronger appeal to Liberals – rose first and asked: 'Will the Liberal Government give votes to women?' No answer came. I joined my voice to hers and our banner was unfurled, making clear what was our question. The effect was explosive! The meeting was aflame with excitement. Some consultation among chairman and speakers ensued and then the Chief Constable of Manchester, Sir Robert Peacock, genial and paternal in manner, made his way to us and promised us, on behalf of the platform, an answer to our question after the vote of thanks had been made. We accepted the undertaking and again we waited. We gave him our question in writing. The vote of thanks was carried. Sir Edward Grey rose to reply without one word in answer to our question! The bargain thus broken on his side, we were free to renew our simple question: 'Will the Liberal Government give women the vote?' The answer came then – not in word, but in deed. Stewards rushed at us, aided by volunteers and accompanied by loud cries: 'Throw them out!' We were dragged from our seats and along the centre aisle, resisting as strongly as we could and still calling out: 'Will the Liberal Government give women the vote?'

Christabel Pankhurst

Violence answered our demand for justice. Yet better violence than jeers, sneers, or silent contempt. Equality was ours that night, we felt, for the force used against us proved that our question was a thrust which had touched the new Government-to-be in a vital spot. The meeting was in frenzy. We were being dragged nearer to the platform which we must pass before our captors could get us behind the scenes. With more than all my strength, resisting theirs, I could stand a moment below the platform. I looked into Sir Edward Grey's face, eye to eye, and asked him again: 'Will your Liberal Government give votes to women?' I remember thinking that, suitably wreathed and attired, he would have looked exactly like a Roman Emperor. Pale, expressionless, immovable, he returned me look for look. I was swept away through the side door, which muffled the deafening tumult in the hall. A revulsion of feeling came in the audience as we disappeared from view. There were cries of 'Shame!' and of sympathy with the questioners. In deference to this, Sir Edward Grey said he was not sure that unwittingly he had not been a contributing cause of the incident which he regretted. The trouble, he understood, had arisen from a desire to know his opinion on woman suffrage, but it was a question that he could not deal with that night, because it was not, and he did not think it likely to be, a party question. His words too plainly meant that women would not in his opinion ever get the vote!

Outside the auditorium and behind the scenes, we were in the grip of policemen and surrounded by stewards. The matter must not, I knew, stay where it was. The Free Trade Hall protest twenty months before had taught me that. What we had done must be made a decisive act of lasting import. We must, in fact, bring the matter into Court, into prison. For simply disturbing the meeting I should not be imprisoned. I must use the infallible means of getting arrested, I must 'assault the police'. But how was I to do it? The police seemed to be skilled to frustrate my purpose. I could not strike them, my arms were being held. I could not even stamp on their toes – they seemed able to prevent that. Yet I must bring myself under arrest. The vote depended upon it. There could be no compromise at that moment of crisis. Lectures on the law flashed to my mind. I could, even with all limbs helpless, commit a technical assault and so I found myself arrested and charged with 'spitting at a policeman'. It was not a real spit but only, shall we call it, a 'pout', a perfectly dry purse of the mouth. I could not *really* have done it, even to get the vote, I think. Anyhow, there was no need, my technical assault was enough.

But how awful it was to read in the newspaper next morning, and I could not and dare not explain the entirely technical and symbolic character of the act, because the magistrate might have discharged me and the political purpose in view would not have been achieved. Even after I came out of prison I was afraid of explaining and so seeming to weaken or recant. It was a great comfort when some person wrote of me as a spitfire. That seemed to show a certain approach to discernment of the real fact.

Annie and I, to make assurance doubly sure, were as militant as we could be, in speaking to the crowd outside the hall. The police dragged us off, followed by a veritable procession of members of the audience. 'What would your father have said to this?' asked one policeman reprovingly. I thought I knew what he would have said. Then a light dawned on another policeman: 'Why, this is what they have been aiming at!'

Arrived at the police station, we were uncompromising and duly defiant. The charge against us must, we were resolved, be entered, and it was. We refused to be bailed out, lest the vital chain of events be broken. Not anxious, it seemed, to display the wretched hospitality of the police cells, they sent us home without bail, adjuring us to appear next morning at the Police Court. We assured them that we should be there!

Mother was anxiously awaiting us and we told her all. Next morning we found that the long, long newspaper silence as to woman suffrage was broken. So far, so good.

Mother came with us to the Police Court. We shivered rather on entering. Police Courts then were associated in my mind only with the sordid and discreditable. However, we were there. A benign magistrate, who had known Father, was not at all severe! But we gave him not the least chance or excuse to let us off. To prison we went.

We had certainly broken the Press silence on votes for women, that silence which, by keeping women uninformed, had so largely smothered and strangled the movement. This newspaper silence had, at the same time, protected politicians from criticism of their offences, omissive and commissive, against the suffrage cause. Mother and I – in the pre-militant days – called on the editor of one of the most important newspapers in the country, asking for the publication of a leading article drawing attention to a Woman Suffrage Bill. The editor, we found, was away; an associate received us. Mother put her request. 'I cannot do this without the editor's authority,' he told us, and went on to explain that in all his twenty years' association with this newspaper its practice had been, as far as possible, to ignore the woman suffrage question. But where peaceful means had failed, one act of militancy succeeded and never again was the cause ignored by that or any other newspaper. Weird rumours were heard now and again of newspaper potentates meeting in conclave and agreeing to be blind and dumb concerning the doings of the militants, but the rumours were false or else the agreements broke down.

Suffragettes leaving Holloway.

2 In small groups make notes on the following:

a) What details has Christabel included which Alan Plater has left out?
b) What changes has Alan Plater made to the order of events?
c) Try to think of as many reasons as you can for the differences between Alan Plater's version and Christabel Pankhurst's.

3 Look at the parts of Christabel's account that refer to the effect the protest had. The incident received three lines in a long account of the meeting in the *Manchester Guardian* on the following day.

a) Why do you think this was?
b) Discuss whether you think Christabel Pankhurst's disruption had as much effect as she claims.

4 Imagine that television existed in 1905. In pairs, plan a storyboard for a news report on the meeting. Where do you think such an event would be placed in a news programme? How much screen time would it receive?

Annie Kenney – Biography

1 Use the information in the play and on pages 44–7 to fill out the following chronological table of Annie Kenney's life.

1879	Born in Oldham. Fifth of eleven children.
1889	Begins work in the cardroom of a cotton mill.
1892	______________________
	______________________
1905	______________________
Spring	______________________
Summer	______________________
Oct 13	______________________
Oct 14	______________________
Oct 17	______________________
Oct 20	Protest meeting after the release of Christabel Pankhurst held at Free Trade Hall, Manchester.
1906	
Jan	Moves to London
Feb 16	______________________
May 19	With others, addresses mass meeting in Trafalgar Square.
June 21	Annie Kenney and two working women sentenced to six weeks imprisonment after trying to call on Asquith, the Chancellor of the Exchequer.
Oct 23	Arrested outside Parliament.
1908	
Feb 13	Takes part in unsuccessful attempt to lobby the Houses of Parliament. Emmeline Pankhurst arrested for the first time.
Spring	Appointed organiser of Suffragette activity in the West Country.
1909	
Summer	Campaign of civil disobedience and attacks against unoccupied property begins. Suffragette prisoners begin going on hunger strike.
1913	
Mar 25	The Prisoners' Temporary Discharge Act (the Cat and Mouse Act) is introduced to prevent Suffragette hunger strikers being given unconditional discharge.
Apr 9	Arrested.

Jun 9/17	Tried for conspiracy and given a long prison sentence. Released after hunger striking.
Jul/Aug	Defies Cat and Mouse Act and escapes to address meetings.
August	Goes abroad with Sylvia and Mrs Pankhurst.
Oct/Nov	Returns to England. Speaks at meetings between periods of imprisonment, eventually from a stretcher.
1914	
Jun 16	Attends a meeting at the Holland Park Skating Rink in disguise. £15 000 raised.
Aug 10	All militant activity suspended after the outbreak of the First World War. All Suffragette prisoners unconditionally released.
1918	The vote given to all women over 30.
1924	Annie Kenney published her *Memoirs of a Militant.*
1928	Universal suffrage for men and women over 21 introduced.
1953	Annie Kenney dies.

2 In groups discuss why you think Alan Plater has chosen to focus on Annie Kenney at the beginning of her militant career.

3 Discuss what view of Annie Kenney you have at the end of the play.

4 Using the information given above, your knowledge of the play and the information given about Suffragettes on pages 52–3 attempt to dramatise another part of Annie Kenney's life. You could improvise at first and then either write a script or prepare a storyboard for television production.

Before you begin discuss what attitude to Annie Kenney you wish to present to your audience. Is she to be a working-class heroine? A hardened militant? A fighter against injustice? A still-idealistic activist?

Hyde Park, June 21, 1908.

Annie Kenney

Attitudes to Women

Intelligence

'It is generally admitted that with women the powers of intuition or rapid perception, and perhaps of imitation, are more strongly marked than in man, but some at least of these faculties are characteristic of the lower races, and therefore of a past and lower rate of civilisation.' [Men, on the other hand, are characterised by rational thought.]

Charles Darwin, 1870

Political Activity

'One never sees any pretty women among those who clamour for their rights.'

Marie Corelli, novelist, 1907

Motherhood

Rock-a-bye baby, for father is near,
Mother is 'biking', she never is here!
Out in the park she's scorching all day
Or at some meeting is talking away!
She's the king-pin at the women's rights show,
Teaching poor husbands the way they should go!
Close then, your eyes; there's dishes to do.
Rock-a-bye baby; 'tis pa sings for you.

Monthly Herald, April 1898

Marriage

'It is a man's place to rule and a woman's to yield. He must be held up as the head of the house, and it is her duty to bend unmurmuringly to his wishes with the due respect his sex demands.'

Anna Sewell, *Woman and the Times we live in,* 1869

Education

Oh pedants of these later days, who go on undiscerning,
To overload a woman's brain and cram our girls with learning,
You'll make a woman half a man, the souls of parents vexing,
To find that all the gentle sex this process is unsexing.
Leave one or two nice girls before the sex your system smothers,
Oh what on earth will poor men do for sweethearts, wives and mothers?

Punch, 10.5.1884

Work

'I have defined Ladies as people who did not do things for themselves. Aunt Etty was emphatically such a person. She told me, when she was eighty-six, that she had never made a pot of tea in her life; and that she had never in all her days been out in the dark alone, not even in a cab; and I don't believe she had ever travelled in a train without a maid.'

Gwen Raverat, *Period Piece*, (Faber)

Voting

The Queen

The Queen is most anxious to enlist everyone to join in checking this mad, wicked folly of Women's Rights, with all its attendant horrors. . . . Women would become the most hateful, heartless and disgusting of human beings were she allowed to unsex herself; and where would be the protection which Man was intended to give the weaker sex?

Queen Victoria, 1870

1 Work in pairs and look at the quotations and pictures above and opposite. Take each in turn and discuss what attitudes to women they show.

2 What evidence of these attitudes can you find in the play?

3 Imagine that you are the editor of an Edwardian newspaper. Write an editorial article commenting on the first London meeting of the WSPU at the Caxton Hall and arguing against votes for women. You may use the evidence presented above as part of your argument.

4 Discuss in pairs which of the attitudes you identified (in question 1) are still voiced today.

A Militant Campaign 1: Suffragettes

The first public meeting in support of votes for women was held in Manchester in 1868. However, despite continuous support for women's franchise both inside and outside Parliament, throughout the rest of the nineteenth century little real progress was made.

This lack of constitutional advance lead frustrated campaigners, most notably Emmeline Pankhurst and her daughters, to adopt a militant policy. The term Suffragette was applied to this group by *The Daily Mail* in January 1906.

Suffragettes chained themselves to railings, heckled political meetings, systematically smashed windows, bombed empty property and refused to pay taxes. In 1913 they bombed the home of Lloyd George, the Chancellor of the Exchequer. One woman, Emily Davison, threw herself under the King's horse at the 1913 Derby and was killed.

Many Suffragettes were imprisoned and were force-fed when they went on hunger-strike; under the notorious 'Cat and Mouse Act' they could be repeatedly released to regain their health and then rearrested. In spite of almost ceaseless activity and great self-sacrifice on the part of the Suffragettes their campaign aroused much indignation, as well as sympathy, and no legislation to extend the right to vote had been passed by 1914.

The Suffragettes' struggle was called off on the outbreak of the First World War. Attitudes to women were changed by the part they played in the war effort and a limited franchise was granted to women at the end of the war in 1918.

Mrs Pankhurst arrested in 1914.

Arson attack on MP's house.

The police battle with Suffragettes at Constitution Hill.

Below is a record of a typical week of attacks on property which followed Mrs Pankhurst's imprisonment.

April 3 Four houses were fired at Hampstead Garden Suburb. Three women damaged the glass of thirteen pictures in the Manchester Art Gallery. An empty railway carriage was wrecked by a bomb explosion at Stockport.

April 4 A mansion near Chorley Wood was completely destroyed by fire. A bomb exploded at Oxted station.

April 5 The burning of Ayr racecourse stand caused an estimated three thousand pounds' damage. An attempt to destroy Kelso racecourse grandstand was also discovered.

April 6 A house at Potters Bar was fired. A mansion was destroyed at Norwich.

April 7 An attempt to fire stands on Cardiff racecourse was discovered. Fire broke out in another house in Hampstead Garden Suburb. In the ruins of Dudley Castle the Suffragettes charged one of the ancient cannons and caused a shattering explosion.

April 8 'Release Mrs Pankhurst', was cut in the turf at Duthie Park, Aberdeen. The word 'release' was twelve feet long.

April 9 A haystack worth a hundred pounds was destroyed near Nottingham.

1 Study the resources on this page. In groups discuss whether you think it is right to resort to violent action in support of political or other objectives.

A Militant Campaign 2: Animal Rights

Baby hurt as animal researcher escapes blast

By Christian Wolmar

A BOMB that exploded under the car of an animal researcher in Bristol yesterday severely injured a baby being pushed near by.

Animal rights activists are believed to have planted the device under the passenger seat of the red VW Golf. It blew a 2ft hole through the floor of the car.

The driver, Dr Patrick Headley, of Redland, Bristol, was not seriously hurt and was able to leave hospital after treatment in the casualty department. The 13-month-old boy, John Cupper, suffered shrapnel wounds and burns and had a finger partly severed. Last night, after undergoing two operations, he was said to be in a satisfactory condition although he may need further surgery. Shrapnel the size of a 2p piece was removed from near his spine.

The boy was being taken in a pushchair by his father, James Cupper, to his mother in Bristol Royal Infirmary. Last night Mr Cupper, 31, said: "I think it is the most callous thing anyone can do. I don't know who it was, but what did they want to do? Kill little children?"

A witness, Keith Malone, who arrived on the scene immediately after the Cotham blast, said: "I just don't know how the driver got out of the car without injury. He was extremely shaken."

Police said later that anyone in the passenger seat would "probably have been killed outright."

Dr Headley is a psychologist and he is employed as an animal researcher working on sheep at Bristol University. In February 1989 the university was the scene of the first bomb attack by animal activists using explosives rather than incendiary devices.

The second attack using explosives happened last Wednesday when the car of a vet working for Porton Down, the Ministry of Defence chemical and microbiological research establishment, blew up as she left her home near Salisbury. Responsibility for that attack was admitted by a caller to BBC South in Southampton who said he represented an animal rights group.

The Independent, 11 June 1990

Joanna Lumley demonstrating against testing on animals.

Animal rights protesters releasing beagles from a laboratory.

Police and animal rights demonstrators clash.

Animal Aid members act out mock sheep shooting outside a defence establishment.

1 What similarities can you see between the present Animal Liberation Front's campaign and the activities of the Suffragettes from 1905 to 1914?

2 Simon Jenkins, the editor of *The Times* newspaper, said in an interview on Radio 4 recently that responsible newspapers should not report the activities of extremists who were using violence to publicise their cause.

In groups discuss whether you agree with Simon Jenkins. How true is it to say that the knowledge that violent actions will be reported if the media encourages these violent activities?

Suffragette Publicity

The great breakthrough that Annie Kenney and Christabel Pankhurst made when they were imprisoned was to end press silence on the issue of votes for women. During the next eight years Suffragettes continued to keep their campaign in the public eye, as the resources on this page show.

A stands for ASQUITH who sought the back door!
B for the BANNER he cowered before.
C for his CONSTABLES, "stalwart" and strong,
D DEPUTATION they hustled along.
E's for EQUALITY, fearlessly taught,
F's for the FRANCHISE so ardently sought.
G's for the GOVERNMENT, "Liberal," they say
H is for HOLLOWAY, gloomy and grey!
I's for IMPRISONMENT, borne for the cause,
J's not for JUSTICE, when men make the laws!
K is our KEY to the door that's still barred,
L's for the LOBBY – they've doubled the Guard!
M's for those MEMBERS, so deep in our debt!
N's for the NOTHING they've done for us yet.
***O**'s the "ODD OBBY," we'll ride till we drop!
P's PARTY PROMISES giv'n as a sop.
Q is the QUERY "Are these tactics the best?"
R's the RESULTS which we show as the test!
S stands for "SUFFRAGETTE" – world-wide renowned!
†**T**'s for TAXATION with TYRANNY** crowned.
U's for the UNION at 4, Clement's Inn,
V is the VOTE we're determined to win.
W's for WOMAN, marching on to the light,
X her X-CELSIOR, heard on the height.
Y stands for YOU, join us 'ere the hour's past, because
Z is for ZANY, who's always the last!

Jan. 1907.

*COMMENT BY A POLICEMAN: "Well, it's an odd 'obby!"
†** "Taxation without Representation is Tyranny."

From a Suffragette poster.

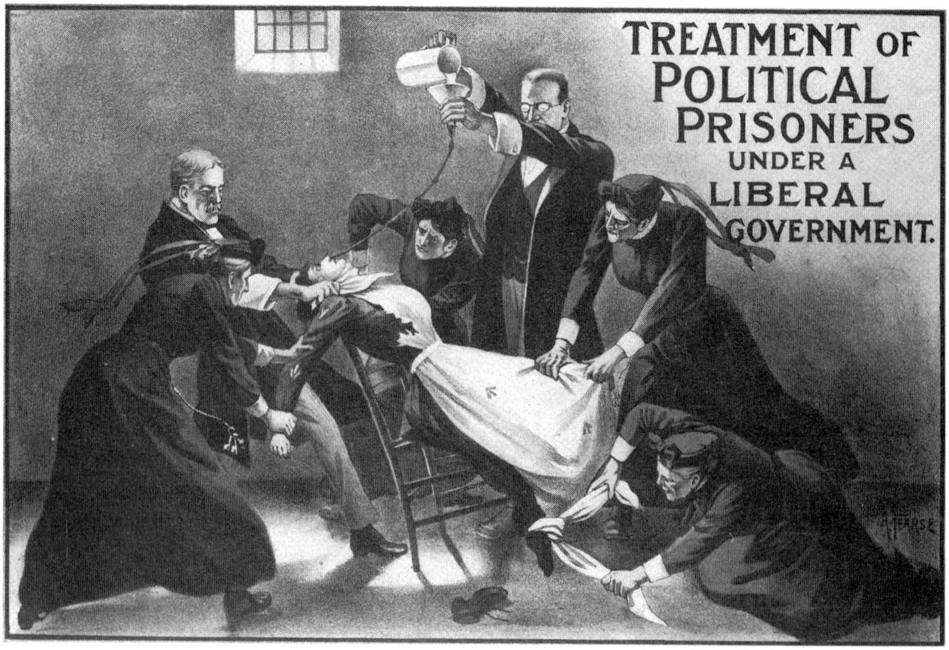

1 Design your own poster or A4 leaflet to publicise the cause of women's suffrage. You could choose to work either in the style of the period or use modern advertising techniques.

Before you begin decide on the balance of textual and visual material you wish to use and on whether you wish to concentrate on positive aspects of the campaign or on the brutal treatment received by Suffragettes.